Druidism

Druidism Guide for Beginners

Druid Overview, Basics Concepts of Druidism, Druid Gods, History of Druidism, the Inner and Outer Path Works, Druid Festivals and More!

By Riley Star

Foreword

Druidry is an ancient belief system and spiritual tradition that can be mapped back to thousands of years. Druidism finds it core beliefs in the preservation and or healing of nature. Their beliefs revolved around the principles of respect toward nature and everything in it.

The purpose of leading a druid life is to love, create and gain better wisdom in all that is around us. Druids, as a whole, share similar ideologies, beliefs and traditions but like everyone, we carve our paths. A druid's path is founded on the ground that all life is interconnected.

You will, as you delve deeper into the topic of Druidism, discover that there are in fact many images, symbol, festivals and such that seem to trace its roots back to Druidism. As you study Druidism further, you may realize the similarities of many of the rituals and festivals with Druidry and many of the religions of the world today.

Table of Contents

Chapter One: History of Druidism

There is perhaps no other group of people who roamed the earth who are as enigmatic as the druids were. Druids have been a mystery that continues to slowly unravel and reveal itself as the discipline is learnt by the ovate. There is more knowledge of today's modern Druids than there is about the ancient Druids of when the world was younger. Information available about the Druids of Yore is second hand information by some of the scholarly writers of before. This chapter will give you the history of how Druidism came about.

Druidism in Ancient History

Early Druids are said to be high-ranking, influential individuals, these is a tribe who are concerned about nature, harmony and balance of the natural world.

It is said that respect for all beings and the environment these beings inhabit are to be revered and respected. Simply put, Druids were a group of priests of the Celtic tribes that lived in Britain and they were very influential, their word given high respect and honor, within the society of the Celts. You could say that they were sort of the upper-crust, especially elite advisors, healers, educators, litigators and arbitrators amongst Celtic tribes.

They were set apart within the Celtic tribes because they formed schools of learning where teachings were passed on rote to students who were interested in the traditions of the Druids. A druid could study the disciplines of Druidism for a very long period of time to later on become the dwelling place of traditions of the people, the stockage of information of communal wisdom in relation to the natural world around us.

They also graduated to becoming the oracle between gods and men, charged with officiating over rituals, and sacrificial offerings.

Druids, regardless of where they could be found, in Britain, Gaul, other parts of Europe and select portions of the Middle East, shared one thing in common. They were revered by the tribes they were part of and are often compared to Magis and Brahmans. They were devoted to prophetic art. They were dedicated to gathering wisdom in nature and in general. They were the repository of tribal information and the link to the gods.

Druidism finds it core beliefs in the preservation and or healing of nature. Their beliefs revolved around the principles of respect toward nature and everything in it. They extend high regard and veneration for ancestors of the movement who came before them, most especially those who were part of the societies of the prehistoric past. Druids are said to have had tribes in Gaul, Ireland, Britain. Today's practicing Druids come from all walks of life and have evolved in many ways, embracing and combining other belief-practices and religions to the basic precepts of Druidic principles.

The early Druids are said to be worshipers of nature and revere the natural world deeply, but very little is known about these ancient priest of the few Druid tribes of the old world. Many scholars have written about them, but then again, many of these written documentation of their lives, existence, belief systems and lifestyles were written mostly by those who tried to over power, oppress, and eradicate the druids, therefore it can't be said if these written text about the first druids are true or if these are misunderstood practices, and the writers misinterpretation of the druids way of living as well as belief system.

Druidism in Europe

Julius Caesar documented much of what he observed of the Druids when Romans came to Gaul. He noted that Druids and noblemen made up the territory of Gaul and that Druids were those who officiated in private and public sacrifices. They were the ones who young men went to for instruction and advice. Druids, Caesar noted, were the adjudicators of quarrels amongst tribe members and they were the ones who carried out judgment and imposed punishment to those found guilty. Those in the tribe who chose to disobey their orders was removed and barred from partaking in any sacrificial ceremonies; the gravest form of punishment that a tribe member can receive.

It is said that only one amongst the Druids was hailed head and chief of the Druids and only upon his death is another appointed in the deceased one's place. There is also information that if there were several druids who were equal in merit, a vote was cast amongst them. Legal disputes were submitted for the Druids to judge once a year, when they annually gathered in a sacred place in what is believed to be the center of all Gaul, the territory of the Carnutes.

Many are attracted by the beliefs and traditions of the Druids also due to the fact that Druids avoided warfare. They also paid tribute to no one but nature and the reverence of the ancient Druids before them. Druids populated because individuals were either attracted by the traditions and rituals or they were sent by their family to study with the Druids.

The training of a Druid was thorough. They were taught the ancient verse extensively. Students of the movement were taught natural philosophy and the science of astronomy. They were given oral teachings of the lore of the gods. Education with the druids was extensive and some took over 20 years of training before they could be called proper druids. The credo and principal doctrine of the Druids was laid on the belief that the soul being immortal, was passed from one person to another upon death. Death was never an issue to be feared because the soul lives again in the form of another person upon one's passing.

It was Caesar who noted that the Druids offered up human sacrifices for those who were gravely ill. They would also offer human sacrifices for those who were in danger of meeting their death in battle. The sacrifices back then must've been an awesome and terrible sight to behold. Druids would sacrifice men by placing them inside of huge wickerwork images which they would later set aflame.

The burning image of the huge edifice filled with usually criminals sometimes innocent men must have been quite an awesome sight to behold. Rites of the druids during the ancient times were held in forest clearings until much later when Roman influence leads them to using sacred buildings.

Apart from Ireland, the Romans, under the rule of Tiberius were able to suppress the Druids of Gaul and later on, Britain. The druids of Ireland, never been influenced by the Romans, lost their functionality as druid priests slowly with the onset of Christianity, but moved on to different functions as poets, judges and historians.

18th to 20th Century Druidism

The first Druids of Britain in the 18th century extolled the ancient Celts and they wanted to keep up the precepts of the old world practices by imbibing the priests or druids of the Iron Age. Now during this time, little was known about the first druids.

The main reason for the lack of information is because teachings were passed down by spoken word. Because of the absence of written text within this society, getting the correct information about druids was challenging and it is safe to say that there was no real connection between the old Druids and the modern Druidic faction no matter the claims of modern druids of the 18th century. During this period, many modern day Druids of that era began forming Druidic association's fashioned organization after the precepts of Freemasonry, using images of the Bards and British Druid as a stamp of its innate British spirituality. In effect the belief was purely one that was romanticized by a group of people who saw this movement as purely cultural and based on community kinship.

Other druidic groups, very early in the 20th century, set out to continue the druid practices by joining movements of those days as naturist societies and the physical culture movement. Naturist were and are known to be individuals who encourages a manner of living that is harmonious with the characteristics that nature intended and features the practice of communal nudity. The movement promotes respect of oneself, and as well respect toward others and the environment. The physical cultural movement of the 19th century focused on strength training and health and owes its origins to cultural trends that were fashionable during those times.

Shortly after the Industrial Revolution, it was thought that middle class members of society suffered from various levels and different diseases brought about by affluence and abundance; the rich lifestyles of the middle class, as a consequence to their wealth to an increasing sedentary lifestyle.

Druids were part of the priestly caste of the Celts and were concerned about matters of religion whilst maintaining a civic role in the society and community wherein they dwelt. These priests, according to scholarly writers, were concerned in the resolutions of disputes amongst individual tribe members. The druids were the ones who were judge and jury to those who committed omissions within the community. They were the ones who judge those who committed crimes, like murder, and who meted out punishments. They too were the ones present during sacrificial ceremonies, and were the people who gave out rewards amongst members of the community.

Excommunication was the highest punishment given by the druids to anyone who refused to follow their beliefs and precepts. Those who were excommunicated were seen as ungodly criminals and were relegated to a life of seclusion. The families and friends of those banished from the tribe were afraid to reach out to the one singled out and separated from the tribe for fear of getting contaminated by the unbeliever. Anyone banished were striped of any rights in the court of the Druids and they would have renounced any and all claims to honor.

The Rise of the Neo - Druids

Along with the rise of the Romanticist movement in 18th century Britain, Druidism once again came into light. This new wave of new age movers extolled the Iron Age Celtic. This new wave of neo-Druids had in mind to imbibe the Iron Age priests of the early druids. Many of the neo-druids claim to possess direct ties to the old world Druids despite the very little information on them and the old world Druids practices. Modern Druids of the late 18th century patterned fraternities fashioned much like Freemasonry, using the image of the British Druids as well as the Bards as icons of spirituality.

These druidic movements of that period were mostly fraternal in basis, focused more on the cultural aspects as they created traditions based on Britain's nationalistic ideals. Even much later on, in the 20th century, Druids of that era joined and merged with movements of that time such as naturists and those who form the physical movement.

Druids joined a lot of other movements that had similarities to the practices of the Iron Age Druids. The 80's saw the rise of a few groups of druids who had embraced the methodologies of the other Celtic pagan tribes, in the hopes of forming druid tribes who would practice druidism more accurately.

The druids were revered personas of the tribe who took on roles as teachers. They were entrusted with wisdom within the commune, describing the traditions of the people and wisdom about the natural world they lived. They were the mediators of and within the tribe, not only amongst themselves, but most especially, they were mediators between the peoples and the gods. Although not explicitly hailed as priests, they did in fact act as such. I

Around the sixteenth century, written text about Druid spirituality and initiation was transcribed by Christian clerics. It describes the magical and spiritual training and awakening of a druid. Christian authors who write about the druids talks about and describes the process of initiation a druid goes through, starting with the druid being consumed by a goddess.

The druid, as ancient writers describes, enters the belly of the goddess and is later reborn as a great orator of words, a poet. The same theme, throughout Scotland, up to the 17th century, is detected throughout the history wherein druids are awakened to the genius of their creativity as poets. In order for them to be awakened to their creativity, they need to be still and lie in darkness for days on end where they are deprived of their senses. It is written that after a period of this sensory deprivation, the new druids are released - or reborn - into the brightness of the earth and the physical world.

Chapter Two: Understanding Druidry

Druidry is an ancient belief system and spiritual tradition that can be mapped back to thousands of years. The first evidence of the druid's spiritual practice is about 25,000 where ancient druids from England, France, and Spain crawled into caves. There on those cave walls are figures of wild animals drawn by those who entered and were initiated in the belly of Mother Earth and were later "reborn" in the light of day. This chapter will provide you with information about the basic things you need to know regarding Druidry or Druidism.

What is Druidry?

The practice of seeking rebirth is found once again about 3000 BCE, when mounds were created wherein initiates would sit in the dark man-made cavern as they await the light and the time for their rebirth. One good example of this man made mounds where initiates would stay the night and wait for the dawn of their rebirth is in Newgrange, Ireland. These mounds said to have been built around the Neolithic period, makes these structures older than the pyramids of Egypt and the great circle of upright stones in Stonehenge.

Here, it was found that the site is made up of chambers and passageways where human bones were found. Many of these mounds, which are surrounded by curbstones that are engraved, and many of the larger stones are adorned with megalithic art. The materials that comprise the monument are materials that had to be exported from as far away as the Wicklow Mountains and the Mournes. Making their work even more challenging than we can imagine given the absence of machinery that would make the work less labor intensive. This gives us an idea of the dedication of the druids to their beliefs and their gods.

It has been the fascination of many not only during the time of its original practices, but was a fascination to many ever since word of the Druids reached the ears of those who imagined them. Druidry is the practice of the learned class of ancient Celtic tribe members. Part of their practices was carried out in the midst of oak forests. These druids were highly esteemed in their circle and were said to be teachers, priests, and judges. They were often thought to hold high ranking positions within the tribe and sometimes superseded kings in decision making.

They were the peacemakers amongst the tribe. They were ambassadors who communicated with other tribes and kept the peace. And they were the ones who bridged the gap between humans and the gods. They were the medium of "communication" between the Celtic deities and the people.

Very little is known about the druids and whatever written texts about them we find are text written by their oppressors. Text about them that has survived time was written by non-Druids which make it harder for modern day historians to decipher this period of druid history.

Who Are the Druids?

Historians who are trying to figure out, who druids were, their role and most especially how the roles of druids changed over time, are greatly challenged because of the lack of first-hand information. Second hand knowledge which is documented by those who oppressed the druids isn't exactly the best source of information about them but it is from them that we discover a tiny bit about the druids of Gaul.

Most of the surviving information about them is principally from Julius Caesar, who conquered them and documented what he observed of the druids. It is said that the Celts appointed those who were devoted themselves to the art of prophecy and general wisdom. The reason for little documentation on Druids and Druidry is because they preferred to teach with passed on wisdom foregoing the act of writing down anything of their precepts. Another writer who wrote about the druids, Dio Chrysostom, likened the druids to the Indian Brahmans and to the Magi.

There is very little known about the Druids or when druidism began. However, giving us a little glimpse of a timeline is Cunliffe, an Oxford scholar, who notes that the earliest reference to the druids date back to about 2,400 years ago.

This only gives us a general idea that druidism started much longer before that, however, we can't say for sure exactly when it was that the druidism began. How far back, we may never know. What we do know is that this was a culture who was an elite, learned group of people amongst Celtic tribes. They were those who possessed great knowledge on astronomy. They had engineering skills that allowed them to construct great megalith structures like the mounds in Newgrange, Ireland. They were thought to have knowledge for Mathematics because of the accuracy of constructions of their monuments, long before the birth of the mathematician, Pythagoras.

Druidism and Christianity

The practice of ancient druidism flourished up to about 1,200 years ago when it was slowly overtaken by Christianity. Today, however, a revival movement of druidism has given new life to the practice. However, Cunliffe, along with other scholars, are careful to remind us about the long gap in between the cessation of the druids of ancient times and the cropping up of revival groups, perhaps owing to the fact that there are little known absolute truths about the druids which lead us to suppose things about them. Take for example Stonehenge. People of today frequently associate druidism to this ancient site. But the mysterious megalithic construction had been determined to date back sometime 4000 to 5000 years ago, in contrast to the earliest documented reference to druidism dates back to around 2400, it is apparent that the gap in between is huge and the missing information is stark.

We still find clues about the druids and their practices, through ancient sources, like the ones aforementioned as well as others like Pliny the Elder, who was born Gaius Plinius Secundus. Pliny the Elder was a

Roman writer as he was a naturalist and a philosopher. He, too, has been one source of information about the elusive druids and their beliefs.

These writers are them who give us a tantalizing glimpse of the life of druids. It is from their reports that we are made aware of their practices and rituals. It is from them that we know that rituals would take place dependent on the season of the year. The mounds we spoke of earlier are believed to be the site of important religious significance because the entrance of the mound is in line with the rising of the sun during the winter solstice. During the winter solstice, the sunlight creeps through a small portal of the mound and floods the inner chambers with sunshine.

The Druids and the Celtic Culture

According to Roman writers, is that druids were either men or women, of great influence in the tribes who developed a highly intricate form of religion. We are made aware that there were three sorts of Druids recognized amongst the Celts and these three classes of druids are the

Bards, the Ovates and the Druids. The Bards were the druids who were familiar with the tribe's songs and stories. Then there were the Ovates, who were the seers of the tribe as they were healers. Then lastly there were the Druids. They were the philosophers of the tribe as they were the teachers, who were commissioned to later pass on their knowledge, and they were judges.

With the coming of Christianity and the Celtic culture merging more and more with that of the Greek and Roman culture, a third period for druids is made apparent by scholars. What were once purposed as schools for the Bards had turned into Christian schools and these operated well into the 17th century. During this period, it is believed that Ovates perhaps progressed on to being the doctors, midwives and healers of the tribe, whereas Druids remained as the learned elite of the tribes and had eventually converted to Christianity.

From the sixth to sixteenth century, the thousand years wherein the Christians triumphed all around Europe, Druid and Celtic spirituality was protected and passed on by clerics of the Christian faith who did the invaluable service of preserving many of the stories and myths through which the spoken teachings of the Druids were passed on. Those who perceive that Druidry died out with the coming of the Christians and Christianity fail to realize that many of the Druid practices are embedded and encoded in the tales of them that continue to inspire the Christian teachings of today. Additional and valuable information about the Druids and the laws in Ireland had also been recorded by St Patrick. It is from his writings that we come to find important details about the social structures of the druids as well as their ethnic standards before the culture of Celtic Christianity took form.

Scholars in Europe by the sixteenth century rediscovered the Druids as they begin to reclaim their Celtic heritage. Through this rediscovery of their heritage they learnt that the information the church had given about the Druids being savages before the arrival of Christianity was far from the truth.

It was also during this period when the Europeans learnt about the Native American people, who were untouched by Christianity and were equally worthy of admiration, provoking a period in which deeper and more intensive studies of the druids and their practices saw a revival of interest amongst the Celts. In fact, William Stukeley, the founding father of archeology, formed a society of Druids in London along with the Princess of Wales, who he referred to as Patroness.

Shortly after, festivals which incorporated Druid ceremonies, as well as the celebration of the Celtic languages of Europe thrived more and more in Cornwall, Brittany and Wales and continued on into the Renaissance period, where even more people are found in Druidry, living in a spirituality of holding everything in nature sacred as it is deeply rooted in the tradition of the elders.

Chapter Three: Druidry and the Awen

The Awen is said to be what true inspiration is. It may originally have been a ceremony directed toward a sun goddess which may have predated the tradition of the Druids. The three lines inside of the three circles may be representative of the goddess of the Sun and Fire, Brighid. The awen is how true inspiration is obtained. Through focusing on the rays and points of the awen, the spiritual and psychic awareness of an individual is opened up the awareness of the person evolves.

Significance of the Awen in Druidism

Many of the druid rituals start and end with the chanting of the Awen. When this is done, the Awen is prolonged, and stretched out to three melodic syllables which come out as "ah-oo-wen". The lyrical tunes of the Awen when chanted this way gives way for the person singing to open up their heart and soul. The Awen is the enlightenment one experiences when the flowing spirit of the Awen awakens their energies. It is the flowing inspiration that stretches out around us and toward the nature that surrounds us.

Awen is the spirit of our being awakening to what is around us, allowing us to open up our spirit or our soul in order for the flow of inspiration to be drawn into us. It is the ability to see beneath the surface and understand as we receive gifts of the divine whether your focus is on nature, or a god or goddess. It is a word that means "poetic inspiration" in the Cornish, Breton and Welsh tongues. Awen in the tradition of the Welsh is the inspiration of Bard poets. An awen can also be a muse of creative minds and artists. Poets are usually described as Awenydd.

Awen can mean rapture or truth in poetic furor. The truth of inspiration and the inspired truth is what Awen can be.

What does the Awen Represent?

Symbolically, the Awen is three lines, often with dots on top of each line, that are interspersed and moves downward and they are drawn within and are enclosed in three circles of varied thickness. It has been explained that the three lines are rays of lights that emanate from the three points of light. The three points of light represent the triplicate of deity. The three dots also represent the Triad of the Sunrises, this being the point, which from the sun rises during the equinoxes and the solstices. The three circles enclosing the downward lines and the dots represent the circles of creation.

In these present times, different neo-druidic individuals and movements interpret the Awen in their own manners relating the three downward lines as earth, sea and air, love, wisdom and truth or body, mind and spirit, stating that the Awen not only about inspiration, but inspiration that has truth and that without truth there is no Awen. Awen, it is believed by many neo-druidic groups are the love of truth, the understanding of truth and the maintenance of the truth.

The Awen is also a symbol that can be drawn by a Druid priest or a priestess to invoke and bring forth good blessings and tidings. While the idea of the Awen and its connection to the sun is frequently regarded as a Revivalist symbol rather than an ancient symbol of Celtic origins, there are druids who believe that the Awen is the translation of spirits flowing is a Celtic symbol that was Christianized.

Examples of these are mentioned in the sixth century Bard Taliesin, who said he was gifted with awen that splashed onto him from the Cauldron of Cerridwen. The Awen is representative of the rebirth to light. Story as such is said to have happened to Gwion, a boy who was said to have been in a shape of a grain and was swallowed by Cerridwen who was a shape of a hen and was after nine months reborn from the womb of Cerridwen as the magician and bard Taliesin.

It was said that Gwion, the foster son of Cerridwen, was stirring the cauldron of Cerridwen when three splashes of inspiration fell on him. This was an explanation that Cerridwen did not find acceptable; she then chased after Gwion the boy, taking on different forms of animals.

Chapter Four: The Gods of Druidism

For the Celts, everything in the natural world had unique significance. The sun god blessed their fields with plenty. The thunder god rumbled in the mountains and beyond and gave rain to the crops. Springs, wells, and placid waters were the dwelling places of spirits and the goddess Danu that were to be appeased with offerings. Outside their settlement was Cernunnos, the god of the animals. The horse that brought them here is the one regarded the highest as the goddess Edpona.

To the Celts, caves, crevices and entry ways to the underworld was a gift of the gods that were meant to be sacred. This chapter will focus on the different Druid Gods and their descriptions.

What are the Druid Gods?

It was the gift of the underworld that underpinned their belief and culture. It was where they found an element worth its weight in gold. Salt was known as the white gold of its time, having the ability to preserve food for long periods of time. They believed in the afterlife and buried along with their dead, as the Egyptians did, their possessions and a boat to use to cross to the afterlife. They also provided the dead with implements the dead would need in the afterlife. Their artistry and ingenuity in the use of iron as casting iron are spellbinding in richness. T

The gods and goddesses of the Druids were those who oversaw the progress of the people and who blest them with bounty and riches. The next section will focus on the different Druid Gods.

Who are the Druid Gods?

Aine is the goddess of love and watched over the summer spells and midsummer rites are dedicated to her. She is the Irish goddess associated with sovereignty and is claimed by many Irish families. Being the goddess of fertility and love she is also associated with crops having command of anything related to agriculture and animals.

Amaethon, meaning ploughman or laborer, in Welsh mythology, was also a god of agriculture and is lauded for being the one responsible for the Battle of Trees. Amaethon is the brother of Gwydion and Arianrhod as he is the enemy of the king of the otherworld, Arawn. Amaethon is also the god of animal husbandry.

Arawn, in the Welsh mythology was the lord of the underworld. It was he who powered those who sought revenge. He was also the god of hunting. Arawn was said to have possessed a magical cauldron that gave way to regeneration. He was also the owner of many hounds; hounds that he would set out to seek out the souls of the dead.

The goddess which influences fertility, beauty, and reincarnation is **Arianrhod**. Her name translated, is a Silver Wheel, which gives the imagery of the ever turning wheel of the year, making her the goddess of the weaving of cosmic fate, time and karma. She is associated with the North Star and the moon making her the goddess of the sky. Her weakness is penchant for vindication and of letting go of the past.

Blodeuwedd, the wife of llew Llaw, came forth through magic by way of nine blossoms. She is the Welsh goddess of wisdom.

Badb is an Irish shape-shifting goddess who is also a warrior. She signifies life and death as she does wisdom and inspiration.

Branwen is the goddess of love in Welsh mythology and her name translates to "blessed raven."

Brighid is the fire goddess in Irish mythology and her name translates to "bright arrow". Tales about Brighid spread was known well in Scotland and England where she is called Bride and Brigantia. She is the goddess of motherhood, learning, inspiration, poetry, and the forge. She influences divination, agriculture and prophecy. Nineteen priestesses keep an eternal fire burning in her honor. She is believed to be a triple goddess.

The goddess which influences and brings about plague, and disease is **Cailleach**. She is a hag that is the complete opposite of the triple goddess, Brighid. Cailleach is the goddess of the biting winter. Her name translated means "veiled one."

Cernunnos is the god of beast, and of the hunt. He influences love and fertility. He is also the god of commerce. He is known as the "horned god" and a god of the underworld.

Cerridwen is the keeper of the cauldron, the goddess of the moon as she is the goddess of magic. She has influence over science and agriculture. She is the inspiration for music, art and poetry. Her name translated literally mean "chiding love". She is the goddess of regeneration being that agriculture deals with the reaping and the sowing of seeds and crops.

Being the keeper of the cauldron, she brewed a magic potion of wisdom and forced Taliesin to mind and stir it for a year and a day. Three drops of the potion came upon him and since then Taliesin grew very wise and was transformed into a Bard. Welsh Bards usually refer to themselves as the sons of Cerridwen. She is the goddess of death and dark prophecy.

Dagda is the god of the arts, of knowledge, music, prosperity and regeneration. He influences fatherhood and is a god of protection. Dagda is also known as the Lord of the Heavens succeeding Nuada as the high lord of Tuatha De Danann.

Danu is the goddess of elements and particularly influences water. She is the goddess of the Earth as she is influential in terms of wisdom and magic. Danu is the well of all life and is the mother of the Tuatha De Danann. She is the most prominent of the mother goddesses.

Diancecht is the god that influences healing. He is the god who fashioned the enchanted well that brings back to life anyone dead thrown into it. But Fomorians later filled this well with stones. Diancecht begot two children. A daughter names Airmed and a son known as Miach.

Druantia is the goddess of the firs. She influences creativity, and knowledge. She is the goddess of passion, is Queen of the Druids and she was who created the lunar calendar. Druantia is frequently linked with motherhood.

Elen is the goddess of paths. She is mentioned in the epic myth Mabinogion where she magically paves vast highways for her soldiers to protect Scotland. Elen is the guardian of the stream underground and unseen from which flows sacred waters.

Epona is the Irish goddess of maternity and healing. She influences prosperity and the protector of horses, mules and donkeys. She is the goddess strongly linked with fertility.

Goibniu is the Irish god of metallurgy. He is associated with hospitality and is known to be a smiting god. He is also known for hosting feasts to the gods. He is said to be the owner of a magical bovine which brings forth abundance. It was Goibniu who fashioned a new arm for Nuada when he lost an arm during a battle. He is the forger of weapons for the gods. He is known to be a great smelter.

Gwyddion is a Welsh mythology god who inspires illusion, magic and enchantment. He is a shape - shifting being. He is the god of inspiration for tuition. Gwyddion is the brother of Amaethon and Arianrhod.

Gwynn ap Nudd is a Welsh god and the ruler of the Otherworld. He is said to be the great "blackened face" warrior. He is the god of death and fallen warriors. He is the god of the international tradition of the wild hunt.

Llyr is the Welsh god of the sea, water as he is the god of the underworld. He is the leader of the warring clans of gods. He is the father of Bran who is the god of Bards and of poetry. He also is the father of Brawen who is the wife of the sun god, Matholwch, the Irish king and Creiddylad.

Lugh is the Irish god who is a member of the Tuatha De Danann. He is a young warrior king and savior to many. He is the influence of learned skills, crafts and the arts. He is the god of truth, the law and oaths. He is often times interpreted as a sun or sky god. In his possession are otherworldly hounds and a magical spear. In his honor, Lughnasadh is celebrated. Tales of the exploits and travels of Lugh are many.

Manannan is god of the sea and influences the weather. He is a sea deity in the Irish mythology and is closely associated with the Tuatha De Danann as well as the Fomorians. Tales about Manannan talks about him possessing a boat called Scuabtuinne or the wave sweeper. The Wave Sweeper is a sea chariot drawn by Enbarr. The sword of Manannan is said to be a powerful sword called Fragarach.

Morrigan is the shape - shifting goddess of magic, prophecy and revenge. She is the goddess of death and war. Morrigan is also known as the Specter Queen and the Great Queen who frequently takes the form of a crow. She is sometimes thought to be a Triple Goddess. She can be known as the maiden called havoc or venomous and can conjure up hatred when there was once none. As a mother, Morrigan is known as Macha and is associated with battle, warfare and cunning. She is associated as protector of horses. She is also known as Badb.

Niamh is the goddess whose name translates as brightness and rdiance. She is the goddess daughter of the sea god Manannan. She is the goddess who rode a white horse which has the ability to traverse across the seas.

Ogma is an Irish and Scottish god of eloquence depicted as a swarthy man with a great ardor for battle. So much so that Ogma needed to be restrained with chains and held back until the proper time for battle ensued. Ogmios is the equivalent of the Celtic god of Gaul and is the god of eloquence. His was the gift of inspiration in the usage of words.

Taliesin is known as the Prince of Song and the chief of poet. He was a renowned Bard believed to have sung in the courts of at least 3 kings. He is the son of Cerridwen. He is one of the semi-mythical beings who are deeply interwoven with the Celtic divinities. He figures in many of the ancient tales of the gods as the boy named Gwion. Gwion was the boy who was told to watch over and stir the cauldron wherein a portion of knowledge was brewing. The potion was meant for the horribly ugly son of Cerridwen. Cerridwen surmised that if her hideous son, Morfan, was a great and wise bard, no one would mind his horrible appearance. Only the first 3 drops of the potion would be effective, the rest of potion would be poison. Gwion, whilst stirring the potion, claimed that he got 3 splashes of the potion on his thumb which he swiftly put in his mouth because the drops were scalding. The first three usable drops of knowledge was then administered, rendering the remainder of the potion in the cauldron, useless unless with intent to kill.

Chapter Five: The Ancient Druids

The religious faith of Druidry amongst the ancient Celtic people from the British Isles and Gaul was prevalent from as early as the second century BC all the way up to the 17th century. The druids of ancient times are a people infused in folklore, legend and mysticism, and so it is not surprising that the ancient druids continue to be an enigma to many. With no written record of their teachings, of their origins and of who they truly were, the ancient Druids remain mysterious.

What are the Ancestors of Druidry?

Generally, the prevailing consensus of them is that they were a highly regarded group of people amongst Celtic tribes of Scots, Ireland, Britain, Gaul and other parts of Europe and possibly Asia.

There are theories that suppose that ancient Druids share ancestry with Eastern beliefs; perhaps this is because they were the only Western movement at that time who believed in the reincarnation.

They are known to be worshipers of nature who went into oak forests to carry out many of their rituals and ceremonies. Druids are set apart from many of the Western religious beliefs in that they are believers of reincarnation. Druids were a highly revered group of people who had divine connection to the natural world who believed that souls were immortal and that the death of a person did not mean the end of that being but a new beginning in the form of another person. Druids believed that once the mortal body dies, the soul or spirit of that person is reborn in the persona of another in the form of a baby or another life form.

Druids subscribed that we exist on two planes. The one we are in now, and the Otherworld, where souls go after their time on this physical plane. They believed that the soul continues to live a life in the Otherworld then dies to be reborn again, back into the physical realm. This is how the Druids believed the cyclical process of trading lifetimes is. During the ancient days Druids were revered as wizened elders of the tribe, they were the link of the people to the gods.

Druids were known to go into oak forests, or would carry out Druidic rituals and ceremonies around oak trees. But one of the many beliefs that the Druids subscribed to and one that we non-Druids have in common is our reverence for those who came before us. In most cultures, whether that is of Western of Eastern origins, one thing that commonly binds us is our innate reverence and respect for those who have gone ahead.

The ancestors of Druidry were the keeper of truths and the walking wells of wisdom and knowledge for the tribes. They were highly respected individuals who came from prominent families of the Celtic tribes who, under tutelage, learnt the wisdom of nature and who linked the tribe members to the gods.

The ancient druids were an order of priests who took care of the tribe and their country. They were the ones who intervened when sacrifices needed to be given up to appease the gods or to influence an event or a situation. They are the special order of people who is able to link man with gods. As caretakers and keepers of wisdom and truths, they were restricted from writing anything down and passed down knowledge to initiates through rote. Only after one has undergone prolonged tuition and probation can he be called a Druid and even after that is sworn to faithfully retain the secrets and mysteries of the movement forever.

The Orders of Druid Priests

The order of the druid priest of ancient Celtic era, like the Magi of Persia, was divided into three categories.

The First Order: Druid Proper

The first or of the utmost nobility in the ranks of Druids were the Druid Proper who were entrusted with the learning, teachings, tuition and rites of the Druid society.

The Second Order: The Bards

The second order of Druids was the Bards who were given the task of conducting public instruction and tuition which they give in verse.

The Ovates

The third class of druids is the Ovates who were given the task of passing on the responses of the gods and goddess to the people who seek their counsel. The Druids had vast, great and deep knowledge of math and astronomy. They had a sense of time and seasons which was part and parcel of the way they worshiped.

Honoring the Druid Ancestors

You will, as you delve deeper into the topic of Druidism, discover that there are in fact many images, symbol, festivals and such that seem to trace its roots back to Druidism. Many of these Druid festivals and important dates, belief systems and such had been renamed or called a different festival with the spread of Christianity. As you study Druidism further, you may realize the similarities of many of the rituals and festivals with Druidry and many of the religions of the world today.

In many different cultures around the world we see something constant that is shared by us all - that is, the reverence of our ancient people and giving honor to them. These ancient rituals and festivals celebrated around the world hold one theme and that is the commemoration and the acknowledgement we give to those who came before us.

Honoring the ancestors has been a mark of the Druids since they were formed in the ancient days and this honoring of the ones before us, is one of the principle beliefs in Druidry that is practiced even to this day by neo-Druids.

Ancestors who lived in the land, who passed on the traditions and stories of the family and those who shared the same bloodline and roots are the first of the ancestors to whom Druids give respect. Honor those who share your DNA and the genetic heritage of the family lines that came before, and this can be seen even with the lay person, or non-Druid.

Blood ancestors are those who carry the hereditary heritage. These are the ancestors who carry the legacy of the family. The lives our ancestors lead are ingrained into our physical bodies and our DNA. They are the ones who worked the earth and built the landscape we now work. Land ancestors are those who originally lived and inhabited the land. They are the ones who opened up the possibilities of the present. The ancestors of tradition are the ones we honor who were the first influencers of the traditions held now.

How to Honor Ancestors of Druidism?

In honor to those who came before us, we now typically commemorate their memories by building monuments. Honoring the Druid ancestor is a tradition that has been passed on for thousands of years and so it is true in these present days. Ancestors are honored by building altars for them. These altars can be indoors or outdoors where the ancients before us are to be paid homage and given food offerings.

Apart from physical offerings such as their favorite food, tobacco or spirit, symbolic offerings, like your time, effort, or energy, may also be offered to those who were before. Another way to pay homage to the ancient druids is by preparing a plate of a tiny feast or a "spirit plate" for them, which is then placed on the ancestors' altar, which traditionally faces the West. Another Druid tradition which is seen celebrated by various forms of pagan movements is the "dumb supper." This is when the ancestors are invited to sup, when one plate is set out for each ancestor invited and one for each living participant.

The present in the physical realm diner quietly sups and tunes in to anything that the ancestors may be conveying during the supper. A cup of mugwort, consumed before divination can help increase the psychic abilities of the one present in the physical realm. Mugwort tea can also be burnt as incense and be used as a visionary herb. The plate of food can be later left at an outdoor altar until the next day breaks.

In honoring the ancestors of our lineage and blood, we can pay homage to the life they led by finding out the most you can about them, where they came from, who they were, what they did. Learning about the history of our ancestors is one way of paying special homage to them. Writing your own history is another way of paying reverence to the ancestors before us. This way when we ourselves become ancestors our offspring and theirs as well will have the documentation of which they can refer back to.

Paying homage to your ancestors can also be in the form of learning or practicing a tradition your ancestors did when they walked the earth. It could be as simple as creating a dish of which the recipe has been part of the family. Perhaps it is a specialty dish that you revive using an old family recipe. Perhaps it is a skill that was prevalent during the time of your ancestors that you can master yourself and practice. This is one other way of paying respects and continuing the tradition of inspired education in actual practice.

Partaking in the conservation of the environment, by reintroducing indigenous wildlife to the wild, by advocating the preservation and upkeep of nature and all within it, we pay deep respect to the ones who before us, took management of the lands and the wildlife in it. Respecting the lands we live in and all that shares the land with us is one other way of showing reverence to our ancestors.

By doing your bit of making repairs on the earth and nature that you and your ancestors may have been a part of is a revenant manner of giving back and honoring your ancestors. We are all guilty to some form or degree of being part of the slow destruction of nature around us. Because of human intervention and occupation of nature, we have become part of the problem. Turn that tide around and be part of the solution as you find ways to help heal the land of the ills it has been fed and subjected.

By tending to the land we live on, we pay homage to those who were before us. Engage in the work they did when they toiled on the lands. Tending to land is one of the best traditions of paying respects to our ancestors. Bringing back the land to its healthy and abundant form, to live amongst nature in a reverential manner, grateful for the provisions of Mother Nature and nurturing these to propagate, not hindering the natural cycle of creation and recreation, is a strong emphasis on upholding the memories and legacy of those before us.

Paying homage to the Druid ancestors of tradition is to be recognized because if not for the ancient Druids and the important ancestors of Druidry, revival and continuity may have ceased. One way of doing this is through reading paragraphs of their writings, if they are available, in sacred spaces, indoors or otherwise. Talking about them in front of the altar and reliving their lives by way of paying respects, is another way of us who are now in the physical realm, to pay honor to them. Knowing where we originate and keeping this sacred body of knowledge we have been given the privilege of partaking is important to recognize. Honoring those who formed these traditions is just and appropriate.

Chapter Six: Sacred Space and Altar Creation

Ancient Druids have been known to be individuals who wear long flowing robes and who go to oak forests and megalithic sites to carry out healing, invoking, and casting rituals. It is believed that by going to these locations, Druids are able to channel the ancients as they are able to communicate with nature and the gods prevailing over Mother Earth. Druid altars are set up in homage for the ancestors. These altars are meant to be sacred spots to be used for ceremonies and meditation and not as a place to worship them. This chapter will provide you with information on how to create an altar for your druidism worship.

Significance of Altar Creation

Altars for the ancestors are meant to be created so that there is a place for the world of living connects with that of the spiritual realm. It is a space where respect and reverence for Mother Nature can be extended. An altar is a place where inspiration is from derived. It is where one can go to in order to connect with the ancients before us. It is where one can ponder their relationship to the divinities and what is around us.

Creating an altar is much like your individual path work. Whilst there is a common ground of beliefs that Druids live by, your walk is also a personal one determined on your belief system and your connection to the Druid gods and goddesses. Therefore creating your own altar will be a personal journey of exploration and discovery. Traditionally an altar, viewed by many world religions is a place where offerings are laid up for intentional purposes.

This too is true in the case of Druidry. However, an altar to a druid is also a place of veneration. The druid altar is an expression of the individual's inner journey. An altar is a good place to set up and visit for your daily meditation practices. It is a place where you can perform rituals as you draw inspiration from the ancient druids of tradition. This is a space where you can channel your inner workings surrounded by objects that would assist you in your inner journey such objects include stones, crystals, and feathers.

How to Create an Altar?

Are you looking to build an altar yourself? You can begin by choosing a space inside your home that you find to be the calmest and most open to the energies of nature. Many beginners choose an altar made of wood which they sometimes decorate with Druidic symbols and imagery by wood burning, a wood art that is common amongst practicing Druids.

An altar is like a representation for most people of their inner journey reflected on the physical plain. Upon the initial setup of the altar you are not expected to have everything on it. Going out to buy "everything" which you think will "go" well with your altar, defeats the purpose of evolution and growth. As you journey through life, you will find little things along the way that you will want to incorporate with your altar. You will receive trinkets and objects that you will deem suitable to place on your altar of meditation.

The purpose and nature of Druidry is to take only what you need from nature. In this age of hyper-consumerism, it is easy for people to forget the core foundation of the precepts of the worship and reverence of nature and overdo things to have the appearance of perfection. In order to work toward the path of being an ever evolving, spiritual and earth-centered people, we need to be very mindful of getting caught up in the consumer race of modern day society.

As advocators of living simply, whatever goes onto the altar has to have very minimal impact on nature. In other words, whatever goes on the altar has to be organic in nature. It should have been given, found, made, or grown. It could be a repurchased made by a local artist.

The energies that these objects bring to the altar should come from a place of intuition and placed on the altar for what it brings spiritually. Keep in mind that objects you bring to the altar will be accompanied by energies of their own originating from where they were from.

Symbology is an important aspect of the discipline of druids and objects chosen by individuals place on their altars pretty much represent energies and places of energies that bring positivity and a deeper sense of spirituality. When you find something during your walks down the beach, like a shell or rock, or when you fancy taking home something you find in the woods, make sure that you have asked nature for permission.

Decorations for a Druid Altar

A druid altar can be comprised of shells or pebbles you may find on the beach. You could adorn your altar with candles which can be lit for ceremonies and rituals, images, or pictures of symbols of the druids, Incense which you can light during meditation, and tools of divination like tarot cards or runes. Many have little bells or chimes which they use to signal the beginning or an end to a ritual. Plates on which to put things like stones, bowls or vessels wherein to place water. You may want to collect representations of the four elements of the earth. You may want to adorn your altar with plants, herbs, beads, objects that have been made by hand, feathers and a journal where you can write your own inner workings and document your journey.

The objects that eventually find themselves on your altar are to represent your inner workings and to inspire you to give reverence to nature and all that is in it. You may want to follow the seasons of the year in terms of adorning your altar. Many incorporate symbols of the season the year is. For example people might set up their altar using the color representative of the season; green and pale blue for spring, a lush green for summer, white, which represents the cold winter months, and gold and a pale purple to represent fall.

Chapter Seven: Druidry and Meditation

Many Revivalist Druids have incorporated meditation in their practice of the ancient craft and religion. The practice and mastering of meditation can be a path to better awareness not only of self but of everything around us. It can accomplish the giving tranquility to the worried heart, it can calm the mind and give peace, it can soothe frayed nerves and rid one of anxiety that ever present in the daily life. Druids use meditation to give honor to the realm that they move in - the physical realm. This chapter will teach you how you can use the concept of Druidry in your meditation.

The Practice of Druidry in Meditation

Druids meditate to go further and deepen their awareness of Nature, its sacredness and its role in the connectivity of all things in the bigger picture of life.

Druids employ meditation techniques of inner journeying in order to deepen their sense of awareness. They meditate so that they get a better sense of being. Meditation is done in a variety of manners which can often include, or be a combination of, focused awareness on the breathing as well as relaxation techniques. Unlike the meditation practices of the East, where the mind is to be released, be rid of and set free of all thought, Druidry is quite the opposite, preferring to train and reorient the meditators thoughts instead of shutting it down.

Druidry recognizes the when reason is separated from reality is just unreal. Western sages, mystics, and even as far back as when Pythagoras reiterated his musings on the matter, all agree that the mind shouldn't have to be the enemy of the spirit during meditation as long as it is brought into harmony with the bigger being of the human, of which it is part of the cosmos. And just like everything else that one wants to perfect, it takes time and practice.

The more you practice this process of the ability to think in a meditative way they better you get at it. Practicing meditation on a frequent basis allows one to become better in the craft of being present at the moment they are in present. Central to this process is being able to ponder meditatively. This form of Druid meditation is what is known as discursive meditation wherein the thinking process is not ceased but instead it is redirected. The thinking process is clarified. It is when the thoughts of the individuals are not obliterated, but it is instead used as a tool geared toward deeper awareness.

The method of discursive meditation usually carried out with the mind initially focused on something specific. Once focused on this topic or image, the mind is allowed to follow out the suggestions and innuendos of the topic using a chain of ideas, whilst keeping the mind focused on and not straying from the image or topic. In this manner the individual slowly changes their train of thought from mindless chatter to a more focused manner of comprehension.

The Process of Druidic Meditation

The meditator's mind first chooses an idea or an image which becomes the theme of the meditation. Once the mind is focused on that chosen image or idea, the meditator then thinks about this theme and allows the consequences and implications of the theme to flow through, harnessing it back when the mind is distracted away from the theme but allowing it free access to follow the theme as far as it goes.

The two positive effects of this sort of meditation teaches the individual mastery of awareness and attention as it allows the meditator to comprehend the themes of which they meditate on in a manner which plain thinking rarely reaches. In addition, the symbols, tuition and myths of the Druid tradition are fashioned especially to bring forth their meaning to the focused and attentive, making discursive meditation a key to the Druid in unlocking the inner dimensions.

There are specific things that one needs to prepare for which will be valuable to their meditation process and the most important of these would be the selection of the theme upon which the individual meditates. There are many symbols and images in the Druid study which can give the individual the theme they seek. These are some of the best themes a beginner can use to focus their meditation on instead of the vast, sprawling topics which can easily throw off the neophyte meditator.

When a new meditator chooses a big theme upon which to meditate, these themes can either cause the meditator to flounder about in the topic they selected or skate over the surface without ever hitting the possible depths of the meditation practice.

As a rule of thumb, if you the theme you choose takes more than a few words to describe then it is too big for a period of meditation to accomplish the job of awareness. You may later on think about breaking up the theme into smaller parts and regroup them later when you have been able to achieve mastery in the simple themes.

Druidic Meditation Guidelines

- Begin your practice of meditation by sitting down on a plain chair without a cushion. Place yourself at the edge of the seat so that your back is not leaned back or propped against the back of the chair. With both your feet on the floor, straighten your back and hold your head upright. Make sure that your back is not stiff, and that your head is not slumped forward.

- Allow your hands to rest on your thighs with the palms faced down and your elbows against your sides. This position allows your energies to be free unlike the Eastern posture for meditation where legs are crossed. This open posture of sitting allows your energies to be open to the rest of the cosmos. This is a vital feature and aspect in the spiritual practice of Druidism as Druids are constantly part of the bigger world around us.

- It is best to face East when meditating, as facing this direction allows you to take advantage of the energies in the Earth.

- Many people find that meditating at the same time of the day and in the same place works toward their advantage. Place a clock in your line of vision so that you complete the meditation cycle without breaking your posture.

- When you have settled into position, make a conscious thought of relaxing each part of your body, beginning at the feet and slowly relaxing the rest of the body part by part until you reach the top of your head. Take the time to focus on your breath. Take a few minutes as you pay close and conscious attention to your breathing.

- When you have given enough attention to your breathing and your [pattern is regular and steady, redirect your attention to the theme of the meditation. In order to do this, speak the theme silently to yourself and visualize it in yourself with a single image, all the while keeping your mind centered on this theme for a spate of time. Begin pondering on the image and the theme and explore it with your mind turning it over and over in your mind as you study the meanings and connectivity of it. Choose a theme that appeals to you and explore the theme as far as it would take you.

- Your thoughts will almost certainly stray from the theme most especially when you are just starting out your training. Contrary to the more commonly known forms of meditation, which tells you to redirect your stray thought back to the theme, the Fourfold Breath meditation technique is quite the opposite.

The Fourfold Breath Method

The Fourfold Breath method doesn't direct you to pull your thoughts back to the theme, but instead, encourages you follow the straying thoughts back to where it left the progression of thought you had been following. Once you are there, proceed to ponder again on the theme and image of the meditation. When you practice this method of meditation you will, in time, find yourself capable of returning to the theme of your meditation as readily as your thoughts divert from it.

The Fourfold Breath is a one of a kind method which allows the individual to salm their body by mindfully regulating the pattern and rate of breathing. It is one of the simplest and easiest methods of the next stage of meditation and is easy to remember. This allows you to remember to focus on your breathing and the counting will bring you back to the task at the moment. The Fourfold Breath is also a method you can employ alongside to deeper workings, much like a warm up before actual meditation. This method is a utilitarian means of achieving rationality and clarity when in a state of panic or when anxious. Consider it a sort of emergency first aid to help clear your head.

The Fourfold Breath Method Guidelines

- Keep in mind that you want to wear loose fitting clothes or no clothes at all, when mastering the Fourfold Breath. You need to make sure that you are able to breathe without constraint as you sit comfortably.

- The first thing to learn with the Fourfold Breath is belly breathing. To do this you want to fully empty your lungs until there is no more air to expel. Inhale deeply and slowly using only the lower part of your lungs giving you the feeling of breathing with your belly, in the general area of your navel. This method of breathing should only make your belly rise and not your chest - much like in pranayama yoga.

- Exhale and repeat. Belly breathing takes time and practice. Allow yourself to learn the proper technique to get the most out of your meditation practice.

- Belly Breathing is the first step to conscious breathing meditation. Once you have mastered the art of proper belly breathing, you will want to move one to learn how to breathe with your chest only taking breaths with the topmost part of your lungs alone. This is not a difficult method to do since this is how most people in the West breathe anyway. Chest breathing is utilizing only your chest and not your belly to take in counted breaths.

- Once you have mastered both methods of breathing, study how to incorporate both chest and belly breathing as you take in a full breath. This time when you breathe, make a conscious effort of filling the lower area of your lungs using the belly breathing method, next you want to fill the utmost part of your lungs with chest breathing. As you release your breath make sure that you fully empty your lungs.

- Lastly study how to rhythmically breathe in a repetitive and fixed manner. This is the Fourfold Breath method, a pattern which is found by many to be effective and is as follows. Inhale and count one to four in a steady fashion. Hold the breath in as you count another four. Counting to four, completely expel the air in your lungs. Then, finally hold your empty lungs to the count of four. Repeat the process until you have mastered this Fourfold Breath method.

Your Body Rhythm

We are all individuals with different body rhythms and it would be beneficial for you to discover your own beat. You may discover that other breath counts to be more effective in placing you in a calm, focused, meditative state. Feel free to experiment on the breathing pattern that suits you best and takes you to place of better equilibrium. You may want to experiment and synchronize your breathing with your heartbeat. Doing so may allow you to get calmer easier.

This may allow you to sink into deeper relaxation faster. Since our minds and bodies are all different from each other, experimenting to discover the best rhythm for you will be the best way to find out what works for you. Focus on doing the Fourfold Breath slowly. This is not a competition to be won. It is a discipline to be learnt through practice and constant awareness. Focus on executing the exercises gradually and being patient with yourself will be key to your success at the beginning.

Learning to employ the skill of the Fourfold Breath especially whilst in the thick of things will have many advantages for you. Once this becomes second nature to you, you will find yourself exercising your abilities to calm down and relax when in stressful situations, helping to dissipate anxiety and tension, thereby allowing you to open up to finding an enlightenment to the event at hand, at the very least, you are able to relieve yourself of the anxiety of the given situation.

Keep in mind that mindful meditation using the Fourfold Breath method allows you to have an emergency go-to when in the throes of a panic attack or when you are plagued by sleeplessness or other tension associated issues. The mere fact of being in the know of a technique that will help you through a rough patch of the day is enough to give you the confidence which in itself could be a life-altering experience.

Chapter Eight: The Druid Festivals and Seasonal Rites

Druid universities were established in order for plebes to study and undergo training to be become fully fledged druids. A druid in training could look forward to and work toward becoming a bard, a priest or a prophet. They were taught through spoken word of lore and they were expected to memorize wisdom, knowledge and teachings which were embedded in folk lore.

This is why brads were important to Druidism. Bards were commissioned to keep historical record through songs. Not only was knowledge preserved and passed on through the work they did through song, songs were considered to contain magical spells to promote a change of mood, sleep, and invoke illness.

Many of these are prayers which are still chanted, sung or said during seasonal festivals of the year. The druid order has been well known for conducting ritualistic ceremonies at Stonehenge for more than a century, during specific times throughout the year of the solstices and equinoxes. They are mindful of the turn of the seasons crucial to inner balance and harmony. Eight times a year, about once every six weeks, Druids come together to take part of celebrations that convey love for nature and the gifts it gives.

It is when people of all ages, from adults to children, would either gather at ancient, sacred sites like Avebury, Glastonbury and Stonehenge or they would congregate in smaller more private groups who would celebrate the changing of the seasons and the cross-quarter festivities of the calendar.

Great love of Nature is the center of the Druid belief and is the heart of the celebrations during the four pastoral calendar festivals.

The Cross Quarter Festivals

The Scottish Gaelic festival of **Samhain** is the most important festival for the Druids because this time of the year signifies the end or the death of the year and the rebirth of a new one. Celebrated on the 31st of October onto the next day of the 1st of November, this period signals the end of the season of harvest and the start of the darker half of the year which is winter. It was religiously observed, throughout Wales, Ireland, Cornwall, Scotland, the Isle of Man and Brittany.

Samhain or Calan Gaeaf as it is called in Wales is when all people avoid crossroads and churchyards as spirits are believed to congregate in these areas and their presence is thick. In Irish mythology this is when doorways to the Otherworld are flung open, giving passage to the souls of the departed and supernatural entities to enter our realm.

Samhain or Calan Gaeaf not only signifies the end of the harvest season and the start of winter, it is essentially a festival meant to honor the dead.

One folklore tells of a women and children who dance around a fire during the eve of Calan Gaeaf. Each villager would then take one stone and write their name on it and put it back in the fire. When the fire gets smaller, before it is out, all the villagers would run home. Staying out later would mean they could be taken by entities of the Underworld in the form of a black sow accompanied by a headless woman. The next day, the villagers gather again to check on the stones. The one whose stone is missing from the lot is doomed to die within the next year.

In other traditions, people would dress up in guise and go around to different houses to ask for food. The disguise is said to set them apart from the supernatural beings, like fairies, which are able to cross into the physical realm and walk amongst people. Death is indeed the central theme of the festival but it does not mean it was a morbid time for the Celts because death to the pagans was not to be feared.

Samhain was in fact a day the pagans looked forward to because family and loved ones who had gone before them were commemorated, celebrated and even invited to the join the living during this feast of the dead.

To the Celts, death meant endings; therefore this was a period when people pondered past relationships, career, jobs and events within the past year. Things that happened good or bad could then be set apart and individuals could move forward.

When the Romans conquered the islands of Britain, the harvest festival for the goddess Pomona was incorporated to the pagan feasts of the Celts, hiding Samhain behind the ruse of All Hallows Eve or All Saints Day, as we now know it. This is evident with the modern traditions we practice presently, although the rest of the original folk lore is pretty much lost with the advent of commercialism. In fact, most of the pagan festivals were concealed behind the Christian festivals of the year, as you will see a little more as we proceed.

Beltane Festival

Celtic festivals are centric on the community and revolve around their needs and because many of them toiled the land and depended on the bounty of harvest, the beginning of the farming year was greeted with much anticipation and hope for a fruitful harvest for the families of the community.

Beltane was a Celtic deity of fire and the festival dedicated to him is celebrated on the first day of May. Beltane is another important day that marks Celtic heritage. This is time when the connection between the living and the dead or the human and supernatural worlds, are eradicated. It is said that on May eve, fairies and witches were given free roam of the land and there was appeasement to be made. Rituals were performed in order to protect community members from malaise.

Beltane is believed to be driving a chariot with the Sun disc. With him he brings, good health and healing. Bel or Belanos is linked to healing springs, wells and waters. He associated with both the solar and aquatic gods. The symbols of Bel include the head with penumbra, a head with a halo, the sunburst, and the wheel.

Festivities during Beltane usually involve fire. Fire is an element that is thought to purify. It is also thought to influence fertility. Cows are passed through fires to ensure a progression of the herd. To bring forth good health, fortune, happiness and fertile minds, bodies and spirits, people of the community would leap over the fire of Beltane to be revitalized and cleansed. Edinburgh boasts off the largest and longest Beltane festivals where crazy celebrations go on until the break of the new day. Think of Beltane when you light a bonfire on the first day of summer.

Lughnasadh Festival

Lughnasadh is the festival druids celebrate at the onset of August and is in honor of the Irish god Lugh. This is the festival hailing the harvest period when fields would glimmer of the corn harvest and when reaping and gathering commences and continues until Samhain. This is festival, celebrated on the 1st of August is usually carried out on top of hills.

It was traditional for people to hike up hills as they gather bilberries, a staple food during the feasts to make as pies and wine, or eaten on the spot. Feasts of Lugh would usually be lavish events of great eats and cake. No festival of Lugh would be complete without the traditional cake called luinean when gifted to a man or luineag, when handed to a woman. This cake is said to be a traditional offering to the gods.

Rituals done during this period, aside from walking up hills and gathering berries, was to go where there were wells, drop in coins or strips of cotton cloth and scatter the ashes from the Lugh bonfires to influence good crops and bountiful harvest. It was a good time to test the waters of marriage and try a probationary one. Couples are given a year and a day to test each other out and when that time is up the couple either chooses to make the marriage official or break it off.

The Festival of Lughnasadh is a good time to go to a garden with your family and meditate about the year of bounty and abundance in your lives. There is always something to be thankful for in pagan practices. Another pagan ritual during this time was the custom of making corn husk dolls from the sheath of harvested grain. The doll is saved until spring when it would be intermingled with the field, consecrating the new seeds set on the earth and ensuring a good crop growth and a bountiful next harvest. This is when pause is considered being on the precipice of the change of seasons as you absorb and imbibe the energies it emits, accomplishing its intended job.

The practice of Lammas is when bread baked from scratch is eaten for the family feast but not before throwing a bit into the fire. Take time to bake some bread with your family and allow them the experience of working with each other. The scent of bread baking will also bring back good memories of good times.

Festival of Imbolc

Celebrated halfway through the winter solstice and the spring equinox is the Festival of Imbolc, which in the Christian calendar is St Brighid's Day, celebrated from the 31st of Jan to the 1st of Feb and is one of the Gaelic festivals observed in Scotland, the Isle of Man and Ireland. Festivals of the same sort in other Celtic lands were happening in conjunction but were called differently.

No matter how the Celts from the different regions called it, Imbolc was indeed a very significant festival during the Neolithic times because it is founded on the alignment of some monumental structures of the land with the rising sun. It is a time when sheep would give birth to new offspring and their teats would be swollen with an abundance of milk. It is a time when the consecration of tools used in the fields were blessed and it marks the midpoint of the dark portion of the year until March 21st rolls around when the season changes and the lands is prepared for renewal and new growth.

Imbolc is originally pagan in its roots but was masked by Christianity and later referred to as St Brigid's Day, a goddess thought to be Christianized by the Romans. Brighid's crosses were fashioned from organic materials and would be brought from house to house.

It is said that Brighid visits the houses of the pagans during Imbolc and so the hosts, in order to receive blessings from the goddess Brighid and for her to protect their livelihood, which would have been the livestock. Food and drink is left out for Brighid and a place where she can rest is laid out as well.

Candlemas Festival

Candlemas is the festival that immediately follows on Feb 2 and is in honour of all virgin goddesses. Candles are lit during this fest and the festival signals the first of fertility festivals which follow.

Vernal or Spring Equinox

Celebrating the renewal of life on Earth in the advent of spring is the Vernal or Spring Equinox on the 20th and 21st of March. It is one of the two equinoxes which are equal in the day and night hours. Today, pagans, as back in the days of Celtic glory, continue to celebrate the coming of spring and are also known as the celebration of Jesus' life, otherwise known as Easter.

The imagery and symbol of the spring equinox are the Green Man and Mother Earth. Mother Earth is said to have given birth to the Green Man. During this time rituals are peppered into the festivities and games of the day as egg races, egg hunts, egg painting and egg eating. Activities of these sorts were alive and well, well before the Christian Easter came along.

Midsummer or Summer Solstice Festival

Depending on the calendar year, the Summer Solstice or the Midsummer Festival happens either on the 21st or the 24th of June each year. Solstice translates to the sun standing still in the sky, which means that it is the longest day of the year with the sun at its maximum limit. Midsummer festivals are celebrated with bonfires which were believed to add power to the energy of the sun.

Pagans consider this time of the year a significant time as it marks the union of the god and goddess who influences fruitful and bountiful harvest for farmers. Pagans sometimes go on a pilgrimage to sacred sites in England to witness the rising sun of the first day of summer.

Autumn Equinox

On the 20th and 21st of September, before coming into days of increasing darkness, the day and night is equal in length and this is when the **Autumn Equinox** is celebrated. This was a time when things slowed down in the expectancy of the coming winter and it was a good period to reflect upon the events that had passed. It was a period to ponder on the change of the seasons, to realize the balance of the year is tipped on its scales. It is interesting for novice astrologers to note that this is the date when the sun enters Libra.

Winter Solstice or Yule

The Winter Solstice or Yule is the celebration of the coming light when the sun begins to draw more of its strength to give. In the tradition of the Celts it was a period when the Oak King defeated the Holly King, which represents the darkness since the onset of Samhain. This time of expectancy for less darkness and more light was something to be grateful for with the assurance of warmth and rejuvenation that comes with the energy of the sun.

It is said that it was during the winter solstice when Heaven's Queen sired forth the Son of Light, and is remembered by the lighting of fires, giving the sun encouragement to triumph over the cold, bitter winter darkness.

Many of the rituals, traditions of the fest, and customs of the winter solstice has been carried over to the more conventional, more Christian way of celebrating. These customs are presently associated with Christian customs, such as homes being decorated with ivy, holly and candles. The yule log from the previous year's oak tree that is set aflame symbolizes the newborn son or the new sun. The mistletoe is another symbol of Celtic traditions that has been carried over into Christianity.

Druids would go deep into the woods during winter solstice, cutting mistletoe's down from branches and catching them before they hit the ground. Druid ancestors would celebrate the rebirth of the Sun King or the Oak King, he who was the Giver of Life, who gave warmth and thawed the frozen earth.

Chapter Nine: Inner and Outer Path Working

As we go through life, we are faced with the many, in fact, too many offerings of the modern times we live in. Today's society has been restructured so radically from even 20 years ago, that it has affected the way we live in such a way that the scale of our values are tipped heavier on one side and it isn't the good side at all. What does this mean for us? People are mainly consumed one way or another in acquiring material things and are focused on getting the latest, the best, the most expensive and the most attractive.

There is nothing wrong with wanting to have the comforts of life and there should be no guilt for those who have the comforts of life available to them. It is how we receive and use these objects for the better you and the betterment of what is around us. These days the outer landscape of the bigger scope of things overshadows the importance of taking care of the inner landscape of our being.

If you pay enough attention, you will notice the gradual shift of the world from the materialism it is consumed with now to a more organic search for meaning, putting value on improving the inner landscape of ourselves. There is no doubt that the outer landscape of our lives is a valuable part of existence but it is certainly not all. Learning how to balance the outer path work with the inner path work is a task that needs attention and mindfulness because life can get distracting.

Developing the Inner and Outer Path Work

The outer path work is pretty much associated with our society that is driven with a masculine spirit. It is the male dominant feature of society that is the take charge, take action kind of attitude. On the other hand, inward reflection and looking into ourselves as we seek to learn our inner workings and path work is the feminine energy. Too much or too little of working on one or the other is a dangerous thing. Each goes hand in hand and one cannot do without the other. We need to find the balance of the go-getting masculine outer path work with the more nurturing, feminine side of our inner path work because it is both of equal value and each have a part to play in the larger scheme of things.

Money is certainly important in order to survive and get things to happen in the realm we exist in but it shouldn't be the sole reason of our existence. If you had seen anyone who has the perks of everything but the other half of what is important in their life is left neglected, it would be obvious to see the disconnect.

To see this in other people's lives is easy, to acknowledge the fall through in our own lives is quite another matter which is why the practice of Druidry directs us to look inward as much as we are focused on the outer path work. It secures us to know that our kin and children have the necessities they require in order to exist and to survive. Material wealth provides us a measure of freedom, choice and the ease of being able to afford things that allow us to live comfortably. In the end it is a useful tool, but is not everything. There is no joy in the money we acquire if we are constantly toiling away and stressing over how to make more.

What is the worth of the material things and the wealth we possess when we pass on? When our soul transcends over, all the money and worldly possessions we have collected over the span of our life time would mean nothing and be of no use to us where we are headed.

Material belongings and worldly assets will not do us any good in the after world life. What is important is that the lesson we have learnt and experiences that has allowed us to understand life on a deeper plane.

Developing our intuition is an important part of our inner path work because our intuition allows us to recognize something that may not be tangible. There are those who are more in tune with the spirit world and have a healthier innerpath work than others but this not make them any more special than the next person. It just means that they have acknowledged the importance of balancing their inner and outer path work and has put in the proper time and attention for both. This can be achieved by anyone who is mindful enough to realize the vitality of the equilibrium of both.

The Inner Path Work

Creating a healthy inner path work is best discovered and nurtured through meditation and silent reflection. Taking the time out to reflect and realizing the importance of looking inward into yourself allows you to open your intuition and frees you to tune in to the spiritual plane around you. It does take time and your mindfulness as well as discipline because the world can often distract us from the important inner work to be done, but with patience and your desire to look inward, you will develop your intuition to be able to recognize subtle cues that is being sent out to you from the spirit realm.

Our subconscious has a way of communicating with us although sometimes vague and encrypted in dreams. Another aspect and feature of the principles and practices of Druidry is learning to crack the code of dreams and what they mean to us.

In simpler terms, the inner path work is the complicated landscape of our emotions. It is our thoughts and feelings which features the relationship we have with spirituality and our association with our deeper, inner selves. It is the notion of understanding something bigger than yourself.

- Our inner path work consists of our beliefs, the foundation of our morals which were instilled to us in childhood.

- Our inner path work is where we store and draw from for creative inspiration. It is also in the inner realm of ourselves where all the feelings we store and carry with us from the past resides.

- Our inner path work is where we can find each and everything that has made us what we have become today. It is where events, experiences and instances of our lives that has shaped us from the manner of our upbringing, the languages we had learnt, speak and spoken to how we were regarded as we were growing.

- Our inner path work is where the experiences and lessons of privilege or exclusion reside. It is where we contain the education and tuition we acquire and learn. It is where the experiences and lessons of isolation or journey lie.

- Our inner path work is where our inner selves reside. It is where the core of our being and all that we have learnt is stored and contained. It is what makes up our person and individuality. This is where we draw from when we feel, think and behave.

The Outer Path Work

The outer path work is a simple deal to explain because the outer landscape is easier to put in words because there are tangible aspects to the outer path work. It is what we see, taste, hear, smell and feel in our surroundings. It is the natural world which we can reach for and touch. It is what has texture and dimension. It could be as broad as the seas or the skies, and the heavens and the heavenly bodies which occupy it. It could be features of the land like mountains, trees, animals. It could be the weather, climate and atmospheric conditions.

Finding the sweet spot of balance between the two is an important aspect of understanding the greater meaning of life and allows us to exist with acceptance whilst honing our intuition on making better choices for ourselves and extending compassion, better tolerance and deeper understanding for those which and who surround us. Druidism is no more a religion than it is a spiritual path with fundamentals laid on understanding the workings of life on a deeper nature.

The Otherworld

Druids get inspiration and feed the spirit from the provisions of nature in this physical realm, but a cornerstone of druid faith is the reality of the Otherworld.

It is a realm that is out of the reach of our physical and worldly senses but it is nonetheless a real place where we go. The Otherworld can be visited during meditation, under hypnosis, or when under a trance of a shaman. It is the place we frequent when we dream. It is also the place to which we go when our soul passes on; it is where our core being goes when our physical bodies die. Druids possess varied insights of the nature of the Otherworld.

Historically, all faiths and beliefs are anchored on the perception that there is another reality which exists beyond the physical realm we move in. Druidism is greatly inspired by Celtic mythology and it abounds with imagery and descriptions of the Otherworld where souls go to in the afterlife. The reality of the Otherworld also solidifies the greatest belief of the druids of yore that the soul is reincarnated and lives through a succession of forms and beings, in animal and human vessels.

Druidry subscribes to metempsychosis wherein a soul transfers from one vessel of physical form to another when the physical body dies. Funerals of the druids focus on the precept that the soul is undergoing transformation – that the soul is experiencing a period of birth and renewal.

Important Qualities of Druids

Ancient druids believe that our soul has to experience a succession of rebirths and reincarnations in order to cultivate deeper wisdom, to experience deeper love and to express the self even more creatively. Having more than one life to live allows us the invaluable opportunity of developing, honing and perfecting these important qualities within us. It gives us the chance to improve the lives we have yet to live and experience.

Wisdom is sought by a person who is more advanced in years. The acquisition of wisdom is mentioned time and again in druid tales and one gleaming example is the story of Taliesin, who was tasked to stir the cauldron where a portion of knowledge was brewing. The importance of gaining wisdom is encoded and embedded in the stories and symbolism of Druidry.

Another aspect central to druidism is the need for **creativity**. Bards, through song and poetry, pass on the wisdom and teachings of druids to the generation after them. Ancient bards are believed to be the keepers of the memories and stories of the community within they live. They are the safe keepers of family lines and genealogies as well as tales which are part and parcel of the landscape of the inhabitants.

It is the creativity of Bards that allow the druid movement to prosper and flourish in these modern times we live. Tales of the Bards give us a glimpse of the Otherworld being a place of sensual beauty where creative artists and talented craftspeople are highly regarded and honored.

Druidry fosters the aim of love in many forms allowing us to deepen our comprehension of love. This third goal of the druids allows us to understand and experience love so as we too can give love freely and deeply. There are many forms and shapes of love and we only have to look around us in order to figure out what it is we love and if that love is applied in the right areas of our lives.

Love of nature and land, the heavens and the wild is one way of druids extolling nature and its bounties. Trees, gardens and groves are integral sites used by druids to communicate with the spirit realm and to receive messages from nature; the love of trees and keeping the land healthy and well maintained is another form of love toward nature and its provisions for us.

Druids are historically and traditionally a peace-loving sort which promotes harmony with everything. The **love of peace** is apparent in druid faith and is displayed during the expression of traditional rituals. Druid rituals always start with peace offerings to each direction of the compass, the love for what is right and just is another pillar of Druidry.

Remember that ancient druids were the judges and jurors. They were the ones who crafted law and were primarily concerned about restoring relations than meting punishment. Ancient and modern day druids encourage the **love of beauty** because it develops the Bard as it fosters creativity and uplifts the artist within us. Druidism encourages the love for all things past and ancient. It promotes a yearning and love for history and respect for the ancients and our ancestors.

Druids have a deep **love for the truth and quest** after it to gain better wisdom and clarity. They are animal lovers and caretakers and respect all forms of life and consider them to be revered and sacred. They have a deep respect for the body and sexuality and consider both to be sacred and not to be messed with. Druids revere the body, sexuality and relationships; not to be confused with piety, prudishness or restraint, real reverence to all three (body, sexuality and relationships) is a strong sensuality as it is kind and gentle.

Druidism encourages a **love for one another by way of community and in relationships**. Druidism promotes that we live a manner of life that is fully committed to living, being and experiencing. It is a spirituality which helps us to be present and fully engaged in life and a passion for living it.

Dreams and Our Inner Path work

Dreams are methods of which our subconscious communicates with us. The younger we are the more perceptive we are of the nature which surrounds us, and we are more in tune (as much as we do not notice and what almost seems like second nature to an innocent) with our intuition. So goes the same for dreams. As we mature, the ability to understand (and follow) our intuition and the recollection of dreams become more challenging.

This is perhaps because of the life society demands us to lead. Perhaps part of the reason why we dream less (or think we do because we don't remember them) is because of the "white noise" in which we are surrounded. We seem to be better connected when we are inspired, when we feed our imagination and create. We are better able to create our inner path work when we find inspiration and are able to listen to our intuition.

People dream all the time, and even those who profess they do not dream in slumber, simply is not "clear" enough in their inner path work to remember them. Perhaps it is because we are bound by jobs that compel us to move immediately after waking which does not afford us the time to languish and take in the moment of wakefulness to remember the dream we had just come out of.

Dreams are another manner of how the spirit world communicates to us and it can reveal a lot about your life, situation and events that are unfolding in your life. Opening yourself up to hone your intuition will go hand in hand with reading your dreams and interpreting their meanings.

Dreams can be vague and confusing to those who have not taken care of their inner path work but they are snippets of messages that give us a glimpse of our inner self and the landscape we have nurtured within. Another way of attaining greater clarity is learning to decipher and understand what our spirit is trying to tell us through the dreams we experience.

Working to focus on interpreting our dreams can give us a few key elements in getting in touch with our inner selves. Finding out the meanings of our dreams, understanding the symbolic imagery of it and being able to define how it relates to our waking lives is one way of understanding the subtle nudges of the spirit world. Our inner path work allows us the possibility of a bigger picture on a wider plane. Make dreaming a meaningful aspect of your spiritual self as you explore the symbolisms of your dreams to the physical implications of it.

Chapter Ten: Walking Your Own Path

We all have our own road to take. We shall be experiencing things in our lives which will influence the way we think, feel, live and react. How we respond to the outer path work should be reflective of our inner path work. Draw on the precept of peace and love from the and adopt a stance that is tolerant of all things with reverence for all, is the goal all druids aim for in this life and the other lives that are eventually experienced. Draw in lessons, experiences and embrace them as you extend yourself to the natural world around you.

Opening up oneself to the occurrences of life and remembering to pay reverence and gift love to people and nature around us, is the goal of druids ancient and now. Druids, as a whole, share similar ideologies, beliefs and traditions but like everyone, we carve our paths. A druid's path is founded on the ground that all life is interconnected.

Neo - Druidism

Neo-druidry is about the interconnection of life and life forms. It is about the connection and connecting with Nature. It is about extending love and understanding and that we are not isolated beings damned to live in solitary, and that we are all, in fact, interwoven and a part of the fabric of life inclusive of all living things and the entire Creation of Mother Nature. It holds everything in Nature sacred and to be revered. You know that you are doing something right when you have a feeling of wellness in the surroundings you live - when you find yourself immersed fully in the life you are intended to live.

The purpose of leading a druid life is to love, create and gain better wisdom in all that is around us.

Exploitation of nature and abuse of what is available to us is an indication of a feeling of separation from the very fabric of one life we are entwined. It is important to note and remember that as much as we carve out our own paths, we are as strongly connected to one another in this life.

Once you understand this that you are a part of a bigger scheme the illusion of being separate falls away and your shrouded vision becomes clearer of life and the gifts nature has for you; when this lie of being alone in the world falls away, then selfishness has no place in your life.

The values and feelings of love become more profound and the benefits not only work toward your favor but it works wonders for society and community as well. When selfishness and the idea of being alone in your journey through life no longer is a part of an individual the reverence for life follows naturally as with the discipline of promoting peace.

Conclusion

Similar to other traditions and beliefs, that, whatever we do in the world, whatever we do to others, creates an effect which also has an effect on us. This is a belief that is held by other faiths, religions, and traditions. From the Druidism, to Christianity, to Buddhism, Hinduism and the Egyptians all believe that 'what goes around comes around,' *Whatever is sown, so shall it be reaped!*

Understanding the greater picture we are part of strips away segregation and awaken us to the truth of the beauty and wonders of nature. This gives us the conscious awareness of how our actions consequently affect, not only others but, ourselves too, in the bigger scheme of things and when this happens we are able to look at life in awe and marvel at the beauty of nature and of each individual we come across. The awareness of harvesting the consequences of our actions (or inactions) dawns on us and becomes a reality we understand to be true. We become witnesses to the process of planting and reaping.

The true test of the value of the inner path work we create leading to an enlightened spiritual path shall reflect on the manner in which it helps us exist in this world we live in. A true spiritual awareness which gives value to our spiritual path is one that gives counsel, provides inspiration, inspires creativity, offers encouragement and extends love in times of difficulty or unfortunate events that are part and parcel of living.

As we mature, we carve different path works in the literal and spiritual realm. Feelings of negativity like panic, anxiety, anger are actual paths that we can make the mistake of continuously traversing. Having an awareness of this can be the first step in choosing to carve out an alternative and totally opposite path work that not only benefits you but nature and the society of which you are part.

Photo Credits

Page 9 Photo by user Xavier via Flickr.com,
https://www.flickr.com/photos/xavier33300/14884844251/

Page 22 Photo by user Chris Funderburg via Flickr.com,
https://www.flickr.com/photos/cfunderburg/4739620238/in/photostream/

Page 33 Photo by user Karen A. Scofield via Flickr.com,
https://www.flickr.com/photos/sari0009/3534725708/in/photolist-6omoNG-ac38Y2

Page 38 Photo by user alisonleighlilly via Flickr.com,
https://www.flickr.com/photos/alisonleighlilly/25218262215/

Page 50 Photo by user anselm23 via Flickr.com,
https://www.flickr.com/photos/anselm23/8556199620/

Page 62 Photo by user Alison Shaffer via Flickr.com,
https://www.flickr.com/photos/skiegazer3/2695922057/

Page 69 Photo by user Barnaby_S via Flickr.com,
https://www.flickr.com/photos/barnaby_s/3521159057/

Page 84 Photo by user Chris Funderburg via Flickr.com,
https://www.flickr.com/photos/cfunderburg/4739621234/in/photostream/

References

"A Druid Meditation Primer" AODA.org
https://aoda.org/Articles/A_Druid_Meditation_Primer.html

"Awen and the Sun" Cassandraeason.com
http://www.cassandraeason.com/divination/druidry/awen.htm

"Celebrations, Festivals and Holy Days"
DruidNetwork.org
https://druidnetwork.org/what-is-druidry/rites-and-rituals/rites-celebrate-seasonal-festivals/celebrations-festivals-holy-days/

"Deep Peace of the Quiet Earth: The Nature Mysticism Of Druidry" PhilipCarr – Gomm.com
http://www.philipcarr-gomm.com/essay/deep-peace-of-the-quiet-earth-the-nature-mysticism-of-druidry/

"Did The Druids Share A Common Ancestry With Other Ancient Religions?" Gaia.com
https://www.gaia.com/lp/content/who-were-the-ancient-druids/

"Druid" Wikipedia.org
https://en.wikipedia.org/wiki/Druid

"Druid Beliefs" Druidry.org

https://www.druidry.org//druid-way/druid-beliefs

"Druid: Celtic Culture" Britannica.com

https://www.britannica.com/topic/Druid

"Druidism/Druidry" Thoughtco.com

https://www.thoughtco.com/about-druidism-druidry-2562546

"Druid Festivals" Druidry.org

https://www.druidry.org//druid-way/teaching-and-practice/druid-festivals

"Druidry (modern)" Wikipedia.org

https://en.wikipedia.org/wiki/Druidry_(modern)

"Honoring the Ancestors of Land, Tradition, And Blood" DruidGarden

https://druidgarden.wordpress.com/tag/ancestor-altar/

"Lughnasadh aka Lammas" Salemsmoon

https://salemsmoon.wordpress.com/festivals-and-sabbats/lughnasadh-aka-lammas/

"Pagan Dreaming" Moon-Books.net

http://www.moon-books.net/books/pagan-dreaming

"Samhain" Wikipedia.org

https://en.wikipedia.org/wiki/Samhain

"Step by Step through A Druid Worship Ceremony" ADF.org

https://www.adf.org/rituals/explanations/stepbystep.html

"The Ancestor Altar" Druidry.org

https://www.druidry.org//library/miscellaneous/ancestor-altar

"The festival of Samhain, Calan Gaeaf, of honouring the dead and the closing of the year" Druidnetwork.org

https://druidnetwork.org/what-is-druidry/rites-and-rituals/rites-celebrate-seasonal-festivals/samhain/

"The Tree Meditation" Druidnetwork.org

https://druidnetwork.org/what-is-druidry/learning-resources/the-tree-meditation/

"What are the Druids' religious holidays or festivals?" Druidnetwork.org

https://druidnetwork.org/what-is-druidry/beliefs-and-definitions/faq/druids-religious-holidays/

"What Is Beltane?" Beltane.org
https://beltane.org/about/about-beltane/

"Your Inner Landscape" The-Guided-Meditation-Site.com
https://www.the-guided-meditation-site.com/your-inner-landscape.html

Feeding Baby
Cynthia Cherry
978-1941070000

Axolotl
Lolly Brown
978-0989658430

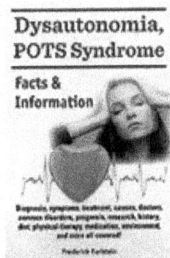

Dysautonomia, POTS
Syndrome
Frederick Earlstein
978-0989658485

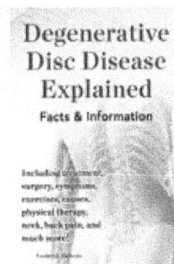

Degenerative Disc
Disease Explained
Frederick Earlstein
978-0989658485

Sinusitis, Hay Fever,
Allergic Rhinitis Explained
Frederick Earlstein
978-1941070024

Wicca
Riley Star
978-1941070130

Zombie Apocalypse
Rex Cutty
978-1941070154

Capybara
Lolly Brown
978-1941070062

Eels As Pets
Lolly Brown
978-1941070167

Scabies and Lice Explained
Frederick Earlstein
978-1941070017

Saltwater Fish As Pets
Lolly Brown
978-0989658461

Torticollis Explained
Frederick Earlstein
978-1941070055

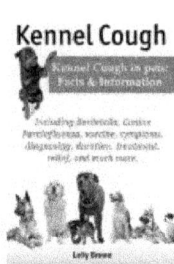

Kennel Cough
Lolly Brown
978-0989658409

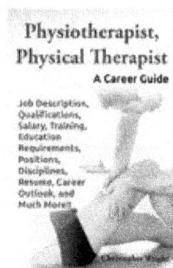

Physiotherapist, Physical
Therapist
Christopher Wright
978-0989658492

Rats, Mice, and Dormice
As Pets
Lolly Brown
978-1941070079

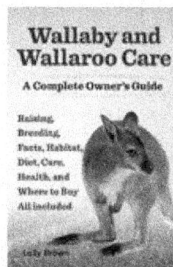

Wallaby and Wallaroo Care
Lolly Brown
978-1941070031

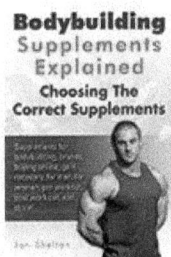

Bodybuilding Supplements
Explained
Jon Shelton
978-1941070239

Demonology
Riley Star
978-19401070314

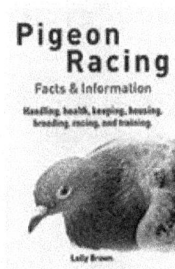

Pigeon Racing
Lolly Brown
978-1941070307

Dwarf Hamster
Lolly Brown
978-1941070390

Cryptozoology
Rex Cutty
978-1941070406

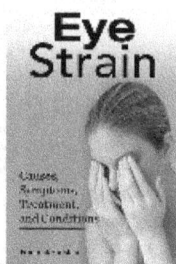

Eye Strain
Frederick Earlstein
978-1941070369

Inez The Miniature Elephant
Asher Ray
978-1941070353

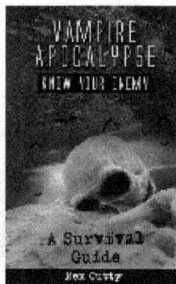

Vampire Apocalypse
Rex Cutty
978-1941070321

www.ingramcontent.com/pod-product-compliance
Lightning Source LLC
Chambersburg PA
CBHW052112090426
42741CB00009B/1779